Horse Basics 101

A look at more than 101 of the most important horse facts every horsey person must know.

Gloria Austin's Collection of Books

Gloria Austin is an award winning preservationist, carriage collector, and holds many championship titles.

www.GloriaAustin.com

ENJOY OUR OTHER BOOKS

- The Brewster Story
- Gloria Austin's Carriage Collection
- A Glossary of Harness Parts
- The Fire Horse
- Horse Basics 101
- The Unsung Heroes of World War One
- The Horse, History, and Human Culture
- Horses of the Americas
- A Drive Through Time
- The Medieval Horse
- Speak Your Horse's Language
- Women and Horses
- The Golden Carriage and the House of Hapsburg
- Horses and Newport
- A Cookbook for Horse Lovers
- Dance! To Improve Riding and Driving
- Hold Your Horses!

Brought To You By The Equine Heritage Institute

Horse Basics 101
by Gloria Austin, President of Equine Heritage Institute, Inc. (EHI)

First Published 2021
Copyright © 2021 by Equine Heritage Institute, Inc.

All rights reserved. No part of this publication may be reproduced, distributed, or transmitted in any form or by any means, including photocopying, recording, or other electronic or mechanical methods, without the prior written permission of the publisher and certain other noncommercial uses permitted by copyright law. For permission requests, write to the publisher, addressed "Attention: Permissions Coordinator," at the address below.

Equine Heritage Institute, Inc.
3024 Marion County Road Weirsdale, FL 32195
Office: (352) 753-2826 Fax: (352) 753-6186

Ordering Information:
Quantity sales: Special discounts are available on quantity purchases by corporations, associations, and others. For details, contact the publisher at the address above.

ISBN: Print 978-1-951895-14-3, E-book 978-1-951895-15-0

Table of Contents

- 10 Foreward
- 11 Define Equine
- 11 Are Horses More like Rhinos than Cows?
- 12 Difference Between Donkeys, Mules and Horses
- 13 Are Mustangs Wild Horses?
- 13 How Many Horses Are There Worldwide?
- 14 What is a Kaimanawa Horse?
- 14 What Is a Foal, a Colt, and a Filly?
- 15 What are the Wild (Feral) Horse Islands?
- 16 What Is the Language of the Horse?
- 16 How Do Horses Greet One Another?
- 17 How Do I Approach a Horse?
- 18 Why Should a Horse be Tied or Kept in a Stall?
- 18 How Long Do Horses Live?
- 19 Do Horses Like to Live Alone?
- 19 Goats and Race Horses
- 20 Why Do We Love Horses?
- 20 Human Brain Chemicals Affected by Horses
- 21 Have These Chemical Interactions Been Studied?
- 22 Why Is the Horse So Popular?
- 23 Royalty and Horses
- 23 Do Horses Prefer to Be Ridden or Driven?
- 24 What Do Horses Eat?
- 24 How Much Water Does a Horse Drink?
- 25 Do Horses Eat Dirt?
- 25 Why Can Horses Drink Muddy Water?
- 26 Can Horses Swim?
- 27 Do Horses Sleep Standing Up?
- 28 Why Do Horses Seldom Lie Down?
- 29 Why Do Horses Stand Outside in the Snow and Rain?
- 30 Why Do Horses Roll?
- 30 What Breed is Best for Long Distance Riding?
- 31 How Long Does it Take for a Newborn Horse to Stand?
- 32 Wearing Blankets and Facemasks
- 33 English versus Western Riding
- 34 What Tools Are Used for Horse Grooming?
- 35 Why Do Horses Wear Bits?
- 36 Do Spurs and Whips Hurt Horses?
- 36 What Makes an Arabian Horse Different?
- 37 What Is a Half Halt and How Is It Useful?
- 38 What is the Fastest Breed of Horse?
- 39 Tallest and the Smallest Breed of Horse
- 40 What Is a Baroque Horse?
- 41 Why So Many Different Colors?
- 42 What Are the Most Common Colors?
- 43 What Are the Less Common Colors?
- 44 Why Are White Horses called Gray?
- 44 Various Horse Patterns and Colors
- 51 Stars, Stockings, Black Points and Blazes
- 59 What Is a Sabino Spot?
- 60 What are Chestnuts?
- 61 What are Ergots?
- 62 Long and Bushy Manes and Tails?
- 63 Does It Hurt to Pull a Horse's Mane?
- 64 What Is a Roached Mane?
- 65 What Are the Gaits of the Horse?

The books created by Equine Heritage Institute are designed to preserve the history and majesty of the horse. Our goal is to find, understand, and pass on the valuable data about equine use and its influence on humanity. The Equine Heritage Institute is a not for profit 503(c) and 100% of all proceeds from the sale of books, services, and products support Equine Heritage Institute's mission.

To make a donation to EHI, please visit www.ehi-donations.com

The Horse

"We have had 6,000 years of history with the domesticated horse and only 100 years with the automobile."
Gloria Austin

66 Which Breeds Are Best At Particular Gaits?
67 Have We Cloned Horses?
68 Foam at the Mouth and Bodies
69 Using Whorls to Identify Horses
70 Spay & Neuter a Horse like Dogs and Cats
71 Poll, Crest, Withers
72 What are the Normal Vital Signs of a Horse?
73 Why Do Horses Use Their Upper Lip?
74 What Is so Special About a Horse's Eyes?
75 Why Do Some Horse Go Blind?
76 Horse's Digestive System
77 What was the Great Horse Manure Crisis?
78 Bones in a Horse's Skeleton
79 Tell a Horse's Age by Looking at Its Teeth
80 Float a Horse's Teeth
81 What are Wolf Teeth?
82 What Does a Horse's Foot Look Like?
83 What Is the Bulb and the Frog?
84 Why Do Horses Need Their Feet Cleaned?
85 Why Do Horses Wear Shoes?
86 Who Is the Farrier?
87 Why Do Horses wear Blinkers?
88 How Much Can a Horse Carry or Pull?
89 How Much Do Horses Weigh?
90 How Do You Measure a Horse's Height?
91 Why Are Horses Measured in Hands?
92 How Do You Estimate a Horse's Weight?
93 Explain the Horse's Weight and Balance
94 Who Are "Horse Whispers"?
95 The Horse Whisperer of the 1800s
96 Rarey and the Queen's Horses
96 Was It Really a Secret?
97 Contemporary Natural Horsemanship
98 Alternative Health Treatments for Horses
99 Why Do Horses Crib, Pace, and Bite?
100 How Can Cribbing Be Curbed?
101 Why Do Horses Kick or Strike?
102 Why Do Horses Paw?
103 Why Do Horses Buck?
104 Why Do Horses Spook?
105 Difficulty with Horses and Trailers
106 What Does Being 'Cast' Mean?
107 How Do You Extricate a Cast Horse?
108 Why do Horses Return to Burning Barns?
109 What is Colic?
110 What is Sweet Itch
111 Common Ailments of a Horse's Skin.
114 What is "Rain Rot" in Horses?
115 Do Horses Get Fleas?
116 Why Do Caretakers Hate Mosquitoes?
117 Why Do Horses Need De-Worming?
118 What is Eastern Equine Encephalitis?
119 Vaccinations Given Regularly in the USA
120 Vaccinations in High Risk Areas
121 What is a Coggins Test?
122 Horse Identification for Official Purposes
123 What is Microchipping?
124 Other Methods of Identification
125 What Is Stringhalt?
126 What Is a Locking Stifle?
127 What is Roaring?
128 Why Do Old Horses Get Swaybacks?
129 Horse With a Broken Leg Fail
130 Monday Morning Sickness
131 What is 'Tying Up'?
132 Bibliography

About the Author

Ms. Austin is a world renowned horse enthusiast. She is particularly well known as a carriage driver and collector of fine antique carriages. Gloria holds many championship titles in single, pair and four-in-hand driving. She has driven over 17 different horse breeds and she has driven horses in the US, Canada, Europe, and Australia. She holds the North American Four-In-Hand and Coaching Championship in Pleasure Driving for the United States. As an accomplished presenter, Ms. Austin entertains audiences with stories of riding, carriage driving, horses in history, and her travels while visiting horse venues around the world.

Dr. Gene Serra and coachman, David Saunders Accompanying Ms. Austin

Gloria serves as President of the Equine Heritage Institute, Inc. and is the founder of a 355 acre equestrian center. Gloria's carriage restorations have won many awards from the Carriage Association of America. Gloria's mission is to educate, celebrate and preserve the history of the horse and its role in changing lives and shaping civilizations worldwide.

After a rewarding career coordinating government planning of services for the developmentally disabled in upstate New York, Ms. Austin opened the New York City metropolitan offices of Paychex, Inc., a company that provides payroll and personnel services for small-to-medium sized businesses. It was Gloria's passion for horses which brought her to sunny Central Florida to enjoy riding and driving year-round.

The history of the horse has long been Gloria's passion. As we are reminded in one of her informative lectures, "We have had over 6,000 years of history with the domesticated horse and only 100 years with the automobile." She is actively publishing books, many of which focus on the 6,000 years when man used the horses in warfare, transportation, industry, agriculture, and commerce.

Gloria is a member of the board of directors of the Carriage Museum of America and serves as Honorary Director of the Carriage Association of America. She also is a founding member of the Four-in-hand Club and has been an active member of the World Coaching Club (an exclusive woman's organization), the Philadelphia Four-in-hand Club, and the European Private Driving Club. She is one of a very few master's level instructors and evaluators with the Carriage Association of America.

Women and Horses by Gloria Austin. Meet some of the most iconic horse women throughout the ages and explore the special bond that women have with horses.

Foreward

Horse Basics 101 is a compilation of useful and interesting facts about horses. It is based on our current understanding of their behaviors. Since horses do not communicate in the same way we do, it is important for us to understand how they act and why.

Understanding equine behavior is important for both the horsey person and the not so horsey person. Both the lay person and the amateur horse enthusiast can appreciate the horse by reading this book. An understanding of the special characteristics of this animal, which has served man for over 6,000 years, is essential. The horse still provides enjoyment today, through association, riding and driving. By looking at horses and understanding their personalities, one can better understand how they behave, what they do and why they do it.

Define Equine

Equines are mammals, belonging to the family equidae. The genus includes ponies, donkeys, mules, horses, zebras, and asses.

Are Horses More like Rhinos than Cows?

The horse and rhinoceros can eat and run. Horses are like rhinos because they have a single stomach. They are both odd-toed ungulates which are mammals with hooves that feature an odd number of toes on the rear foot.

Horses can survive on lower quality food than cows, but must eat larger quantities. The cow is a ruminant with a decidedly more complex digestive system. Unlike the ruminant, odd-toed ungulates (perissodactyla), have relatively simple stomachs. Odd-toes ungulates are hindgut fermenters, digesting plant cellulose in their intestines, rather than in one or more stomach chambers. In the horse's cecum, a organelle of the intestines breaks down the cellulose in grass.

Difference Between Donkeys, Mules and Horses

- Donkeys and horses are the same family, but different species.
- Donkeys have 62 chromosomes.
- Domestic horses have 64 chromosomes.
- Mules, the result of crossing a female horse with a male donkey, have 63 chromosomes.
- Mules live longer than horses and are noted for having fewer skin, leg, and foot problems.
- The wild Przewalski's horse, the only truly wild horse, has 66 chromosomes. These animals cannot be domesticated or trained to work with humans.

Are Mustangs Wild Horses?

No, Mustangs are feral horses who are descendants of domestic horses with 64 chromosomes who were released or escaped and roam free. Horses wandering free in our American west and on the Island of Assateague that are managed by the US Bureau of Land Management are feral, not wild horses. A true wild horse like the Przewalski are not as trainable and have 66 chromosomes.

How Many Horses Are There Worldwide?

- USA has 10.15 million horses.
- China has 6.77 million horses.
- Mexico has 6.35 million horses.
- Brazil has 5.5 million horses.
- Argentina has 3.59 million horses.
- Colombia has 2.53 million horses.
- Mongolia has 2.11 million horses.
- Ethiopia has 2.028 million horses.
- Kazakhstan 1.528 million horses.

(cited Figures derived from the Food and Agriculture Organization (FAO) of the United Nations, 2011)

What is a Kaimanawa Horse?

Kaimanawa horses are feral horses in New Zealand. They are descended from domestic horses released in the 1900s and known for their hardiness and quiet temperament. A wide variety of heritages has given the breed a wide range of heights, body patterns and colors. They are known for being well-muscled, sure-footed and tough.

What Is a Foal, a Colt, and a Filly?

- Foal – a baby horse of either gender.
- Colt – a young male horse from birth to age 3.
- Stallion – a male horse.
- Gelding – a castrated male horse.
- Filly – a young female horse from birth to age 3.
- Mare – a female horse.
- Broodmare – a female horse used for breeding
- Dam – the mother horse.
- Sire – the father horse.

What are the Wild (Feral) Horse Islands?

Wild horse islands refer to a group of barrier islands off the Atlantic coast where feral herds of horses are still found. Although not technically wild, but escaped, domestic horses allowed to go feral, these horses have survived in these scattered ranges for hundreds of years, some have been around longer than the mustangs of the American West. Below is a list of locations where there are still feral island horses on the Atlantic coast.

- Assateague, MD
- Chincoteague, VA
- Back Bay, VA
- Corolla, N.
- Ocracoke Island, NC
- Shackleford Banks, NC
- Cedar Island, NC
- Carrot Island, NC
- Cumberland Island, GA

What Is the Language of the Horse?

- Snort – a signal of danger
- Blow – to clear the airways when exercising
- Squeal – when strangers meet, excitement, aggression or excitement when breeding
- Nicker – when meeting human friends, often at feeding time, or a stallion's greeting of a mare or a mare for her foal.
- Neigh – to call to another horse
- Whinny – a longing for another horse

How Do Horses Greet One Another?

They stretch out their heads and sniff each other's noses.

How Do I Approach a Horse?

It is best to approach a horse from the front at a 45 degree angle of its front shoulder so he can see you advancing. When approaching a horse from any angle, speak in a soothing tone, so the horse knows you are coming and is not startled.

Often horse hostlers start training in a round pen, so the horse can grow accustomed to taking direction from the trainer's body language at a distance. Handlers will sometimes keep very close to the horse's body; this way they do not take the full impact of a kick. Once gentled, horses do not generally kick.

Why Should a Horse be Tied or in a Stall?

- Since horses take flight, they must be enclosed in a stall, fenced area or tied.
- A loose horse can run in front of a car and hurt itself and others because of its large size.
- Since they sometimes rear backwards when tied, we use a halter and what is called a quick release knot.

How Long Do Horses Live?

The average life span of a horse or pony is between twenty and thirty years. Although according to the Guinness Book of Records, Old Billy was believed to be the oldest horses on record. A he was a Cleveland Bay cross foaled in 1760 who lived to the incredible age of 62.

Do Horses Like to Live Alone?

No, they are herd animals and live in hierarchical groups. Horses without a herd can develop problems. They like to know where they stand (no pun intended). They like a boss and this has been the reason they can be domesticated and take direction from humans.

Goats and Race Horses

Get Your Goat: To make someone annoyed or angry. The expression comes from horse racing. Goats are thought to have a calming effect on race horses. Prior to races a goat was placed in the horse's stall on the night before a race. The goat would keep the horse from pacing and exhausting itself. Unscrupulous opponents were known to steal the goat in an effort to upset the horse and cause poor performance during the race. (cited. The American Heritage® New Dictionary of Cultural Literacy, Third Edition, Copyright 2008 Published by Houghton Mifflin Company. All rights reserved.)

Why Do We Love Horses?

While there has always been anecdotal evidence that "There is something about the outside of a horse that is good for the inside of a man (or woman)," solid, empirical evidence now exists to support this belief. Studies and research show an enhanced link between our brain chemistries ("nurture" psychosomatic response, specifically oxytocin) and the presence of the horse.

What Brain Chemicals Do Horses Affect in Humans?

- Endocannabinoids: "The Bliss Molecule"
- Dopamine: "The Reward Molecule"
- Oxytocin: "The Bonding Molecule"
- Endorphin: "The Pain-Killing Molecule"
- GABA: "The Anti-Anxiety Molecule"
- Serotonin: "The Caonfidence Molecule"
- Adrenaline: "The Energy Molecule"

Have These Chemical Interactions Been Studied?

In a 2012 metastudy,"Psychosocial and Psychophysiological Effects of Human-Animal Interactions," researchers found the following:
- Improvement of social attention, behavior, interpersonal interaction, and mood.
- Reduction of stress-related parameters such as cortisol, heart rate, and blood pressure.
- Reduction of self-reported fear and anxiety.
- Improvement of mental and physical health, especially cardiovascular health.

In the Journal of Traumatic Stress, April 2015, 28, 1–4 a report, titled "Equine-Assisted Therapy for Anxiety and Post-traumatic Stress Symptoms" found the following results: Participants' PTSD symptoms, emotional distress, anxiety symptoms, depression symptoms, and alcohol use decreased significantly following program participation. An article published in April 2012's edition of Research in Autism Spectrum Disorders found: "a 10-week therapeutic horseback riding (THR) intervention with children diagnosed with an ASD can result in significant improvement."

Why Is the Horse So Popular?

- Historically the horse has been valued for its speed. It can be domesticated and allows men and women to go faster than their two legs can carry them.
- It takes wealth to support a horse so, in the past, it was viewed as an animal of the privileged and as such, communicated status.
- The horse has been instrumental for generations in commerce, trade, war, agriculture and transportation.
- It is a cross cultural symbol of beauty, speed, freedom and power.
- It is considered the pivotal animal in the development of civilization.

Royalty and Horses

The Queen and Queen Mother have long loved their horses.

Do Horses Prefer to Be Ridden or Driven?

- This is difficult to ascertain – maybe driven.
- Horses enjoy the company of other horses so they appear to like being driven as a pair or four more than going out alone.
- Riding horses like to go in groups too.
- Under saddle, the horse has an additional task of balancing the rider and supporting the rider's weight.

What Do Horses Eat?

Food
- Grass
- Hay
- Grains

Minerals
- Phosphorus
- Calcium
- Iodine
- Copper
- Magnesium

Ponies and donkeys should be fed less than horses.

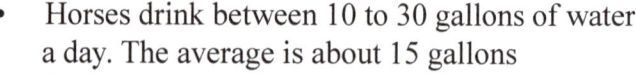

How Much Water Does a Horse Drink?

- Horses drink between 10 to 30 gallons of water a day. The average is about 15 gallons
- Water is vital to equine digestion.
- Sometime horses refuse to drink water when away from home, so it is helpful to add cider or other flavorings.
- Karo syrup, honey or salt applied to the lips and gums sometimes entices a horse to drink.
- Capillary refill and a skin pinch test are helpful to detect dehydration.

Do Horses Eat Dirt?

Horses only eat dirt when they are lacking in minerals. They will eat their own manure if hungry enough, but typically avoid grazing where they defecate. Horses will avoid foods that smell bad, whether from bacteria, mold or dirt.

Why Do Horses Drink Muddy Water?

- Some horses lack needed vitamins and minerals that can be found drinking muddy water.
- Valuable minerals collect along riverbanks and in muddy waters and can be beneficial.
- Stable managers need to supplement the horse with these natural minerals.
- Horses accustomed to warm climates sometimes refuse to drink cold water. Low intake of water can cause digestive and other problems in horses.

Can Horses Swim?

- Yes, swimming comes naturally to horses, but it is hard work.
- Only a well-conditioned horse can swim for 20 minutes.
- A 500 yard swim is equivalent to a mile's gallop.
- Horses should swim in cold water, because of the large amount of body heat generated while swimming.
- Horse owners who swim with their horses should be cautioned not to enter water with anything that might get entangled; such as saddles, harness, bridles, or tie downs.
- Do not go far away from shore, since the horse may become exhausted and not have the energy to return.
- Swimming is used as therapy for limb injured horses.
- Horses will naturally breathe loudly when swimming.

Do Horses Sleep Standing Up?

- Yes, as a prey animal, the horse has this adaptation to escape its predators. Lying down makes it vulnerable, costing the horse energy and time to get up to take flight.
- The horse needs its speed and quick reaction time to flea in the face of danger.
- The 'stay' apparatus, unique to horses, allows it to stand and sleep.
- The 'stay' apparatus is called a locking patella. This apparatus when "locked" holds the stifle and hock in extension. When its "unlocked" the stifle and hock can be flexed.
- Therefore, horses can also stand for long periods of time.

Why Do Horses Seldom Lie Down?

- A horse needs about 30 minutes to lie flat for REM sleep and only lies down an hour or two every few days.
- Horses sleep better in the company of other horses and may become sleep deprived and develop problems if kept entirely alone.
- A single horse should at least be kept in sight of another horse.
- Experienced horsemen look for signs of illness when they notice a horse lying down too long or thrashing when on the ground.

Why Do Horses Stand Outside in the Snow and Rain?

Horses do not like enclosed spaces or shelters because it impedes escape from predators. Horses stand outside in nature. With the exception of severe weather conditions, horses are healthier outside. They possess a dense coat, as well as a layer of fat for protection. As a general rule, horses that live outside in all types of weather, tend to be healthier than those that are stabled. Many horse people keep their horses outside day and night and only bring them inside in preparation for work.

Naturally, during dangerous or severe weather, horses should be stalled to help reduce or prevent injury. A good practice is to braid an identifying tag in their manes. This way, in the event they escape from their enclosure during bad weather, they can be identified.

Why Do Horses Roll?

- The roll is a means of grooming their itchy skin.
- A horse's skin is seven times more sensitive than ours, so more things annoy them.
- After rolling, they shake off excess dirt; the dirt that remains protects them from insect bites and flies.
- A good roll is also equivalent to a chiropractic adjustment or a good stretch in humans.
- Persistent rolling can also be an indication of colic or stomach distress.

What Breed Is Best for Long Distance Riding?

The Arabian – It has been bred for generations for stamina and covering long distances in a short time. Even though they are known for their canter, long distance requires a trot. They, along with other breeds compete in endurance competitions where they are ridden 100 miles in a day.

How Long Does It Take for a Newborn Horse to Stand?

Since being on its feet and taking flight is important to the survival of horses:
- Foals are born within 20 minutes of labor.
- Foals stand and start nursing within the first hour of birth.
- Foals can run within the first two hours after birth.
- As soon as the foal is steady on its feet, the mare will move the foal from its birthing place, because predators soon smell the scents of the birthing area.

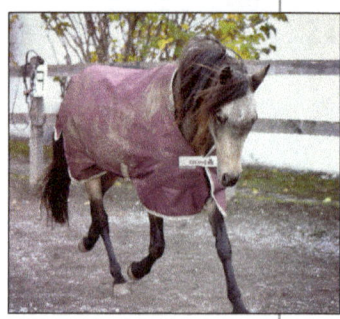

Why Do Horses Wear Blankets, Sheets, and Facemasks?

- Blankets and sheets can protect the horse from the sun, rain, snow, or sleet.
- These coverings act as a constant groomer – keeping out dirt and stroking the hair as the horse moves.
- Facemasks are primarily for keeping flies and gnats out of the horse's eyes.
- Blankets, quarter sheets, and coolers can also be used to keep in body heat.
- Cold rain, a bath in chilly weather and resting after sweating on a cold day can cause a loss of body heat so a cooler is often used.

What are the Differences between Western and English Riding?

The difference is more than just the saddle design and different bits.

Western horses are neck reined – one hand on reins.
- Neck reining was originally developed for working cows.
- The horn on a western saddle is for wrapping a rope.

English horses are direct reined – two hands on reins.
- Direct reining is designed for dressage, hunter/jumper work and fox hunting in Great Britain
- English saddles have no horn, because some are meant for jumping.

What Tools Are Used for Horse Grooming?

These are some of the common tools in a grooming kit:
- Stiff Brush
- Soft Finishing Brush
- Curry Comb
- Hoof Pick
- Cloth
- Sponges
- Sweat Scraper
- Fly Spray
- Mane Comb
- Mane Brush

Grooming is a form of bonding and is pleasurable for both the horse and the person. It is a time to also examine the horse for injury and other problems such as skin irritation. The hoof pick is used to remove any lodged particles, dirt and debris from the bottom of the hoof.

Why Do Horses Wear Bits?

- The bit on the bridle is the best way to communicate with the horse.
- Their lips and mouths are sensitive just like ours.
- 60-70% of the horse's weight is in front of the girth and 90% of its balance is in its head and neck.
- The horse's mouth has a naturally occurring place for the bit to rest.

Minuscule movements of the fingers on the reins can direct the movements of a trained horse. Simple, properly timed, gentle tugs can affect the balance of the horse enough to move its foot slightly to the right or slightly to the left.

Do Spurs and Whips Hurt Horses?

- Spurs and whips are used to signal the horse and control the horse's movement.
- They also can be used as a quick way to get the horse's attention to respond in a certain way.
- They are not used as punishment.
- The trainer must develop trust with the horse and remain calm at all times.
- The art of horsemanship is about being clever and figuring out how to get this big animal to do what we ask.

What Makes an Arabian Horse Different?

Most horses have 18 ribs, 6 lumbar vertebrae and 18 tail vertebrae. Arabians usually have 17 ribs, 5 lumbar vertebrae and 16 tail vertebrae

What Is a Half Halt and How Is It Useful?

"The half-halt is the hardly visible, almost simultaneous, coordinated action of the seat, the legs and the hand of the rider, with the object of increasing the attention and balance of the horse." [USEF Rule Book DR108]

- They work because 90% of a horse's balance is in its head and neck.
- Collection is the engagement of the hind quarters to create impulsion through to the front quarters.
- Through collection, the horse's body becomes balanced over its legs.
- When this occurs, the slightest of tugs on the rein can shift the balance of the horse.

What is the Fastest Breed of Horse?

The Thoroughbred, developed in Great Britain is the fastest horse. The highest race speed recorded over two furlongs is 70.76 km/h (43.97 mph) and was achieved by a 2 year old filly Thoroughbred, Winning Brew.

Secretariat set and still holds the world's race record. In June 2012 the Maryland Racing Commission, using a forensic review of the race, determined that not only had Secretariat set a course record in 1973, he had been even faster than previously believed—1:53 flat.

As noted in Equine Vet J Suppl. 2006 Aug;(36):128-32. *Racing speeds of Quarter Horses, thoroughbreds and Arabians.* Despite similar race times reported for 402 meters, Quarter Horses averaged faster speeds than Thoroughbreds when timed from a standing start. In short races, both breeds accelerate throughout the race. Arabians, despite being known for endurance, had slowed by the end of the race.

What Is the Tallest and the Smallest Breed of Horse?

The Shire Horse of Great Britain is the tallest and heaviest of the horse breeds.
- 'Sampson' was 21.2hh and weight 3,360lbs.

The smallest horses in the world are the Falabella miniature horse of Argentina.
- Silver Flash was a prize-winning stallion at 28 ½ inches tall.

What Is a Baroque Horse?

Baroque Horses can be dated by various works of art starting in the 1600s. They are characterized by elegance, beauty, arched necks and long flowing manes and tails. The Baroque horse was originally a war horse, developed in the age of the bladed weapon. With the advent of gunpowder in warfare, the Baroque horse was divided into battle wagon pulling breeds and high speed breeds.

According to Baroque Horse International Magazine, Baroque breeds include:

- Frederiksborg
- Friesian
- Kladruber
- Knabstrupper
- Lipizzan
- Lusitano
- Mangalarga Marchador
- Menorquín
- Murgese
- Mustang (Spanish)
- PRE (Spanish)
- Warlander

Why Do Horses Come in so Many Different Colors?

Color perhaps developed in horses due to survival of the fittest. Dun color (for reasons of camouflage) seems to be the color of the horse left in the wild in the open range. White is the predominant color in arctic areas, and dapple gray in the European forests. Humans have, through selective breeding encouraged other color's and we have developed an advanced understanding of breeding for color.

What Are the Most Common Colors?

- Bay
- Brown
- Chestnut
- Gray

What Are the Less Common Colors?

- Albino (lethal in horses) (red eyes at birth)
- Appaloosa
- Black
- Buckskin
- Champagne
- Cream
- Cremello
- Dun
- Grulla (a type of dun)
- Palomino
- Perlino
- Pinto
- Paint (a Pinto with Quarter horse or Thoroughbred bloodlines)
- Roan
- Silver dapple
- White (yellow or blue eyes)

Why Do Horse People Call White Horses Gray?

- Most white horses are gray because they have black skin pigment under white hairs.
- A true white horse will have white or pink skin under white hairs.
- Gray horses are usually born dark and lighten with age.
- Steel, dapple, flea-bitten and rose are often used to describe various types of gray horses.

Marked by the progressive fading of the base color, Gray is not considered a base-color, neither is it a dilution, rather it is a gene which removes pigment from the coat over time. Considered the strongest coat modifier, it acts upon any base-color. Once the hair is de-pigmented, the horse's base coloring never returns.

The White Horse

Truly white horses are born pure white and retain their pure color throughout their life. A truly white horse has a lack of pigmented skin and a white hair coat. Generally white horses have dark eyes or blue eyes. Certain white horses are born with some skin and hair pigmentation, this coloration may be retained into maturity. In contrast, grays retain skin pigment and only the hair becomes white over time.

Dominant White

Dominant white is best known for producing pink-skinned all-white horses with brown eyes. One of the parent must have the dominant white gene. Dominant white does not "skip" generations because it is dominant. Dominant white, while rare, occurs in many breeds. Dominant white horses commonly have white noses which are more prone to sunburn.

Albino Horses

Some breed registries call certain white horses albino, but technically this is incorrect. According to William Castle, in his *The ABC's Of Color Inheritance in Horses*, "There is no reported case of a true "albino" horse, despite references to white horses that are called "albino". All horses that are called "albino" have pigmented eyes, usually brown or blue, so they are not true albinos. Albinism occurs when a foal receives one recessive gene from each parent.

Lethal White Overo

Frame Overo is a certain genetic marker and considered highly desirable as a white pattern gene. However when both parents carry this marker, the foal has a likelihood of being born with Lethal White Overo syndrome and will die shortly after birth.

Leopard

The leopard complex is characterized in the Appaloosa and Knabstrupper breeds with spotted coats. The few spot leopard pattern, however, resembles white. These horses are called white born in some parts of the world. White born foals are less common among Appaloosa horses than Knabstruppers or Norikers. Homozygous leopards are prone to night blindness.

Palomino

The Palomino has a body which is golden in color, varying from bright copper color, to light yellow, with light mane and tail. True Palominos have no black points.

Pinto (Coloured In The UK)

Pinto coat color consists of large patches of white and any other color in random patterns. Pinto horses have a variety of defined patterns including:

- **Piebald** – Base coat of black with various colorations.
- **Skewbald** - Any base color other than black with various colorations.
- **Overo** – White over dark patterning not crossing the back.
- **Tobiano** – Rounded white patches crossing the back, lacking jagged patches.
- **Tovero** - Have a "war bonnet" around their ears (Dark pigmentation) and are dark around their eyes, one or both eyes will be blue, and their dark markings will be more isolated and spread out on their body.

Roan

Roan coats have white hairs evenly intermingled throughout any other color. The head, legs, mane and tail have fewer scattered white hairs or none at all.

Cremello

Cremellos have pink skin and blue eyes. Their hair coats are not white but are of a light creme color. Cremellos will have white manes and tails.

Perlino

Perlino horses have cream coats with pink skin and blue eyes. The manes and tails are often darker for perlinos than for cremellos, often described as coffee colored, or as having a yellow or tan cast.

Grullo/Grulla

Grullo is a dun horse with tan-gray or mouse-colored hairs on the body. There are several shades, referred to with a variety of terms, such as black dun, blue dun, slate grullo, silver grullo, silver dun, or lobo dun.

Stars, Stockings, Black Points and Blazes?

COLOR PATTERNS OF HEAD

Star
A star is designated by a small, clearly defined area of white hairs on the forehead.

Snip
A small patch of white which runs over the muzzle, often to the lips.

COLOR PATTERNS OF HEAD (continued)

Stripe
A long narrow band of white working from the forehead down toward the muzzle.

Blaze
A white stripe down the face to the lips.

Bald Face
One which has white over most of the flat surface of the face, often extending toward the cheeks.

LEG MARKINGS

Leg markings are generally described in relationship to the highest point of the horse's leg that has white coverage.

Coronet - white strip covering the coronet.

Pastern - White from the coronet, including the pastern.

Half Pastern - Only half the pastern is white.

Ankle - Extending from the coronet up to and including the fetlock.

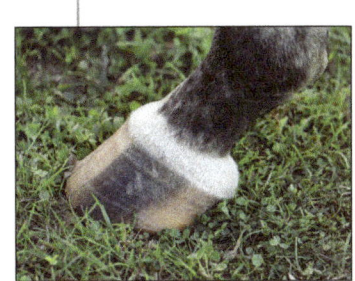

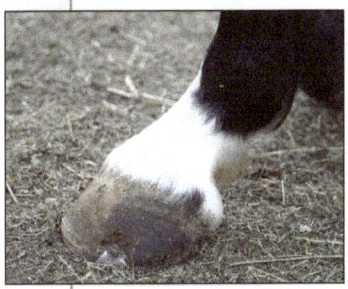

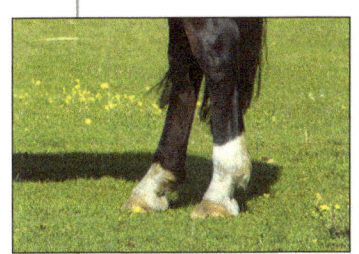

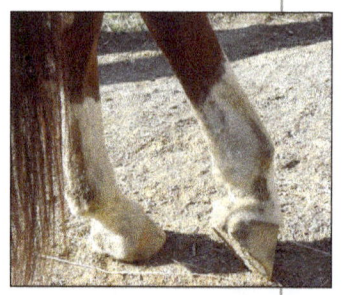

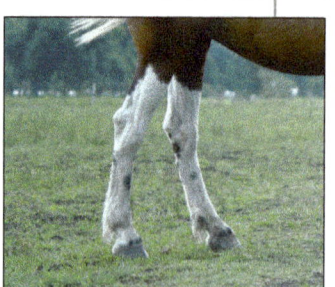

LEG MARKINGS (continued)

Half Stocking or Sock or Boot - From the coronet to the middle of the cannon.

Stocking - white marking that extends at least to the bottom of the knee or hock, sometimes higher.

Full Stocking or High Sock - From the coronet up to and including the knee.

Some additional terms used to describe leg markings.

Irregular: Often used to describe certain types of stockings with irregular patterning.

Partial: Describes an incomplete pattern, most often a sock or other short markings.

"High White": White stockings which extend above the knee or hock, characteristic of the sabino color pattern.

MANE AND TAIL

The term **"Black Points"** indicates a dark mane and tail.

The term **"White Points"** or **"Light Points"** indicates a light mane and tail.

Flax or flaxen is a straw yellow or dirty white mane and tail.

Silver is used to denote a mane or tail which is white with a few black hairs giving it a silver cast. *White manes and tails have only white hairs or they are silver.

Rat-tailed is a horse having little hair in its tail.

Broom-tailed or Bang-tailed refers to a heavy, coarse tail.

PRIMITIVE MARKINGS

Primitive markings in foals - Foals may exhibit many of the primitive markings listed below, which later fade or disappear completely. This tendency is more common in buckskin, smoky black or black foals.

Dorsal stripe - A dark stripe down the back of a donkey, mule, or horse. Present in all primitive breeds of horses, though it is not exclusive to primitive breeds. All dun horses possess some vestige of a dorsal strip.

Zebra bars - A common addition to the dorsal stripe, most often seen on or above the knees and hocks.

PRIMITIVE MARKINGS (continued)

Shoulder stripe - A vertical marking, usually seen across the withers and extending down the shoulders.

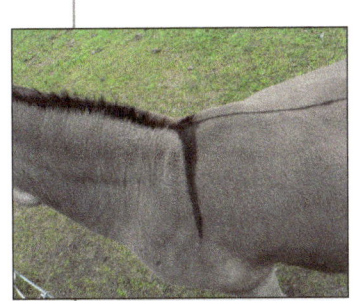

Cross - Combination of the dorsal stripe and the shoulder stripe, when both are prominently visible is termed a cross. Often seen in donkey breeds with wild African ancestry.

Dorsal barbs - Vertical striping on either side of the dorsal stripe, also called fish boning.

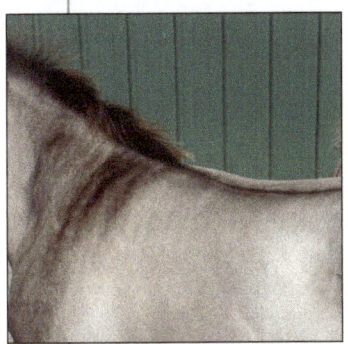

Rib marks - Fine, faint stripes sometimes responsible for horses being classified as brindle.

OTHER PRIMITIVE MARKINGS

Ventral stripe - Line running along the mid-line of the underbelly.

Zippers - Paler lines of hairs running vertically along the back of the animal's leg, usually from the hoof to the knee. Found where horses often have feathering, considered by some to be guard hairs.

Cobwebbing or spiderwebbing - Fine, radial stripes on the forehead.

Face masks - Darker hair on the lower half of the face.

Ear marks - Dark markings on parts of the ear, the rim, the back half of the ear, or striping on the back of the ear.

Ear tips - Tiny white or paler tips on the ear.

Eye spots - Rare, often across the eye, over it, or under it.

What Is a Sabino Spot?

White spotting patterns in horses.

A wide variety of irregular color patterns are accepted as sabino.

What are Chestnuts?

- Horney or callous-like growths located just off the knee on the inside foreleg and hock of the horse.
- Either vestiges of toepads.

They are unique to each horse. Chestnut is also a hair coat color.

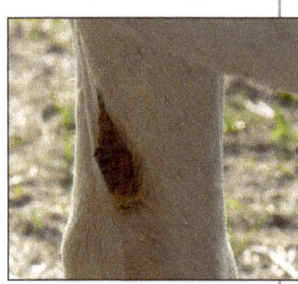

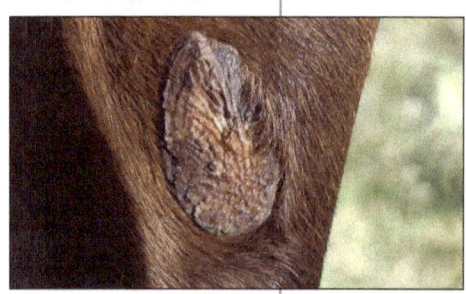

What are Ergots?

- Ergots are horney or callous-like growths located just at the back of the fetlock.
- They can be found on both front and rear legs.
- Ergots can be trimmed without hurting the horse.

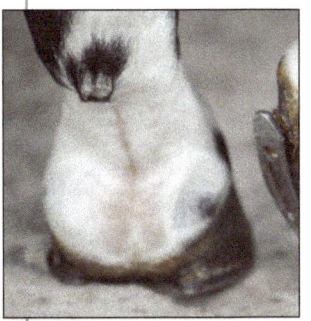

Why Do Some Horses Have Long and Bushy Manes and Tails?

- Genetics dictate the individual characteristics of the horse.
- Draft horses and Baroque horses tend to have more and longer mane and tail hairs.
- A horse's mane hairs are untangled with fingers, not by a comb, which would break the hairs.

Does It Hurt to Pull a Horse's Mane?

- No, horses have no nerve endings at the base of the mane.
- Eventing, dressage, and hunter/jumpers trim manes to about 4-5 inches and do about 13 braids along the top line of the mane.
- Braiding helps prevent the mane from getting caught in the rider's hands which is important for the rein release while jumping.
- Braiding and trimming keep the horse cooler.
- French braids do not generally require mane pulling.
- Pulling and braiding a horse's mane is considered an art, and some styles require specialized skills.

What Is a Roached Mane and Why Is It Done?

- Sometimes referred to as "hogging" the mane, this refers to completely shaving the mane.
- Roaching is commonly done for polo, polocrosse and roping to stop entanglement with the hands, polo stick and rope.
- In some countries, mares' manes, forelocks and upper tails are roached.

What Are the Gaits of the Horse?

Walk
- The slowest
- 4 MPH
- A four beat lateral gait

Trot
- The most sustainable gait
- 8-10 MPH
- A two beat diagonal gait

Amble
- Designed for riding
- 8-10 MPH
- A two or four-beat lateral gait

Canter
- A three beat gait
- 10-15 mph

Gallop
- A four beat gait done at differing cadences
- 40 mph

Which Breeds Are Best at Particular Gaits?

Walk (the gait of the agricultural horse)
- Drafts such as Belgium, Clydesdale, Percheron

Trot (the gait of the driving horse and warhorse)
- Morgan, Saddlebred, Welch, Friesian, Andalusian

Amble (the gait of the comfortable saddle horse)
- Paso Fino, Missouri Foxtrotter, Tennessee Walker, Rocky Mountain Horse

Canter (the gait for fast sprint work of racing or herding)
- Quarter Horse, Thoroughbred, Arabian

Have We Cloned Horses?

Yes, in 2003, Italy's Laboratory of Reproductive Technology created the world's first successful horse clone, named Prometea. Since then, the following champions have been cloned.

- Show jumper 'ET'
- Endurance horse 'Pieraz'
- Quarter Horse 'Royal Blue Boon'
- Barrel racing 'Scamper'
- Cutting horse 'Tap O Lena'
- Dressage champion 'Rusty'

Polo star Adolfo Cambiaso with six clones of Cuartetera he rode at the Argentine Open.

Why Do Horses Foam at the Mouth or on Their Bodies?

Foam seen at the mouth, means the horse and rider are working the bit properly in the horse's mouth, which stimulates the salivary glands. Foam (or lather) on the body of the horse means the horse is sweating and is expelling excessive heat during exercise.

Why Do We Use Whorls to Identify Horses?

A hair whorl is a patch of hair growing at a different angle to the rest of the coat. The locations that whorls can be found on equines includes; the stomach area, the face, stifle areas, and sometimes on the hocks. Hair whorls in horses are also known as crowns, swirls, trichoglyphs, or cowlicks and can be either clockwise or counterclockwise in direction. Like human fingerprints, each set is unique. Author Linda Tellington-Jones believes a horse's personality and capabilities can be known by reading these patterns.

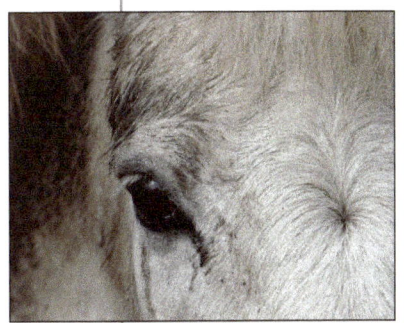

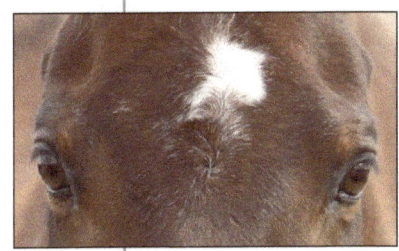

Can You Spay and Neuter Horses like Dogs and Cats?

Stallions in our culture are frequently neutered (what we call gelding). Neutering is most commonly done for behavior rather than birth control. As colts, they are usually castrated by their second birthday. Gelded horses grow taller. Female horses are sometimes spayed. This has been made easier with the use of laparoscopic surgery.

Poll, Crest, Withers

Poll: The top point behind the ears where the top of the bridle rests. The poll is important because correct flexion at the poll joint is a sign that the horse is properly "on the bit," allowing for efficient communication.

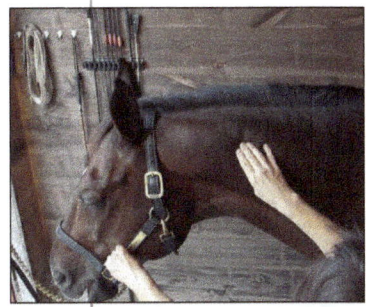

Crest: The upper portion of the neck, where the mane grows. Horses that walk, trot, and amble generally develop thick musculature around this area. Cantering breeds that race, use their necks differently and may not develop such musculature on their top line.

Withers: The ridge between the shoulder blades of a horse, commonly where the mane stops. This is the standard place to measure the animal's height.

What are the Normal Vital Signs of a Horse?

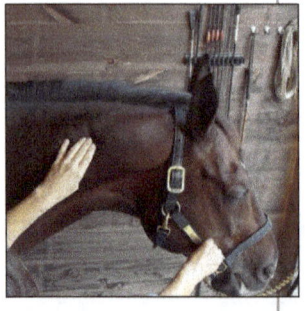

- Capillary refill time – 1-2 seconds, gum color – pink
- Gut sounds – long and short rumbles and gurgles
- Heart rate – 30-44 beats per minute at rest
- Respiratory rate – 10-15 breaths per minute
- Temperature – 99-101° F

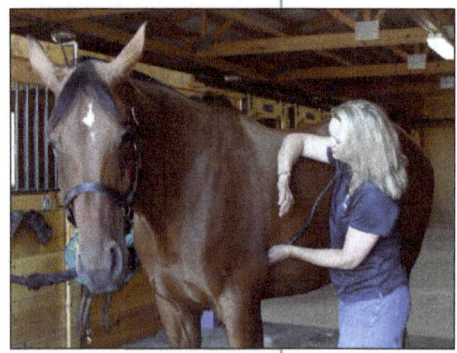

Why Do Horses Use Their Upper Lip so Much?

Horses have a prehensile upper lip adapted for seizing, grasping or taking hold of things. The upper lip is very sensitive and is capable of feeling the smallest of difference in objects. When squeezed with the hand or a twitch, endorphins are released and calm the horse for certain procedures the horse finds annoying.

What Is So Special About a Horse's Eyes?

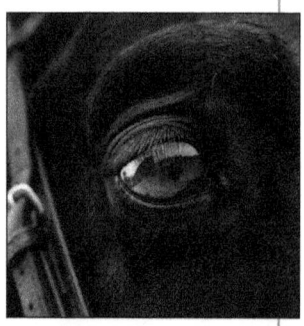

- The horse has the largest eye of all large mammals.
- The horse's 345-degree range of vision makes it well adapted to perceive motion, particularly when its head is down and grazing.
- Only its four legs and its body hamper its view, while grazing.
- Horses have excellent night vision. However, they need time to adjust to changes from dark to light.
- Because their light receptors line up in the middle of their eyes, they often have to reposition their heads to see at a distance.
- The horse has both monocular and binocular vision. (1) Monocular area (2) Binocular area.

*Horses have a blind spot directly in front of them at close distances and another, directly behind them.

Why Do Some Horses Go Blind?

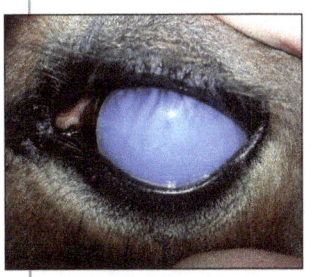

Large eye size creates more opportunity for injury or infection. The cornea has no blood vessels to fight eye infection and injury, so horse lovers need to pay particular attention to the health of the horse's eyes. Uveitis (inflammation of the middle layer of the eye) in horses is called "moon blindness" and is caused by trauma, parasites, bacteria, fungi, or yeast infection.

Horses are susceptible to glaucoma, a condition of increased pressure within the eyeball, causing gradual loss of sight. Cataracts and retinal detachment can also occur in horses. Sometimes an eye has to be removed. Blindness in one eye causes depth perception problems. Owners of one-eyed horses should be aware and use caution when engaged in activities that require depth perception.

What Is Special about the Horse's Digestive System?

- Horses are herbivores or "plant eaters".
- They have one stomach which holds 2-4 gallons of materials.
- Their small intestine is about 70ft. long (a human's is 21ft. long)
- Horses large intestine can hold about 20-25 gallons of plant matter.
- On any given day, the average 1,000-pound horse will produce approximately 50 pounds of manure. This amounts to about eight and a half tons per year!

What was the Great Horse Manure Crisis?

In 1900, there were over 11,000 hansom cabs on the streets of London alone. New York had a population of 100,000 horses producing around 2.5 million pounds of manure a day. Major cities were struggling with the problem of tons of manure, which caused smell, disease and required large amounts of manpower to manage.

Horse manure problems in 19th Century New York City.

This problem came to a head when in 1894, The Times newspaper predicted... "In 50 years, every street in London will be buried under nine feet of manure." The advent of the motor vehicle eliminated this crisis, but brought about the collapse of all the supporting economies, such as farriers, horse breeders and stabling businesses.

How Many Bones Are in a Horse's Skeleton?

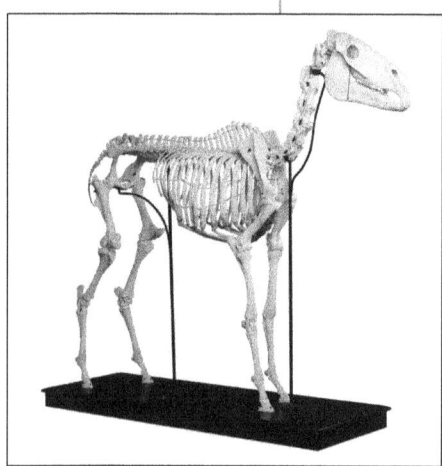

Horses typically have 205 bones. Commonly, Arabians have less, because of having 5 lumbar vertebrae instead of the usual 6, and 17 pairs of ribs rather than 18.

Interestingly, a horse's scapula is attached to its body with only ligaments and muscles

Can You Tell a Horse's Age by Looking at Its Teeth?

Yes, but be careful - their teeth can hurt!
- Experts can tell the horse's age by tooth eruption and tooth angle, marks and wear.
- The bit sits between the incisors and the first premolars.
- Dental work on horses is extremely important.

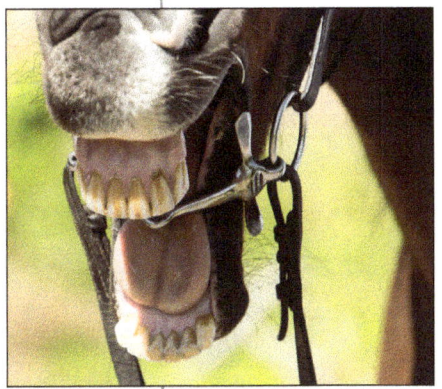

What Does It Mean to "Float a Horse's Teeth"?

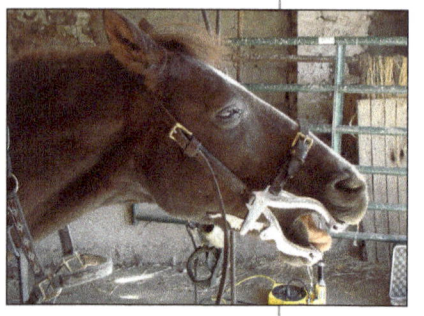

- The teeth of a horse never stop growing Floating is necessary to file or rasp horse's teeth to make the chewing surfaces flat.
- The instrument or file is called a float.
- The speculum is used to hold the mouth open and keep the back teeth apart.

What are Wolf Teeth?

- Wolf Teeth are vestigial premolars, usually on the upper jaw.
- They often cause problems and so are generally removed.
- Mares usually have 36 teeth, and adult male horses have 40 to 44 teeth
- Adult horses' teeth are several inches long and continually erupt through the gum line
- "Interdental space" is the space in the upper and lower jaw with no teeth, this is where the riding or driving bit rests.

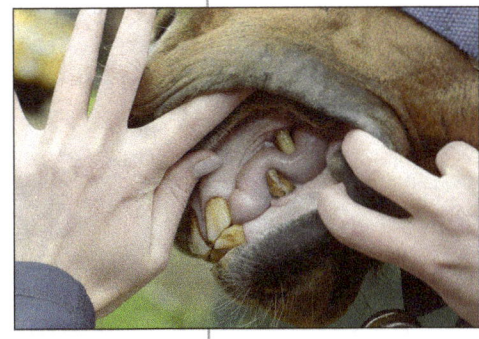

What Does a Horse's Foot Look Like?

BAREFOOT HOOF, LATERAL VIEW

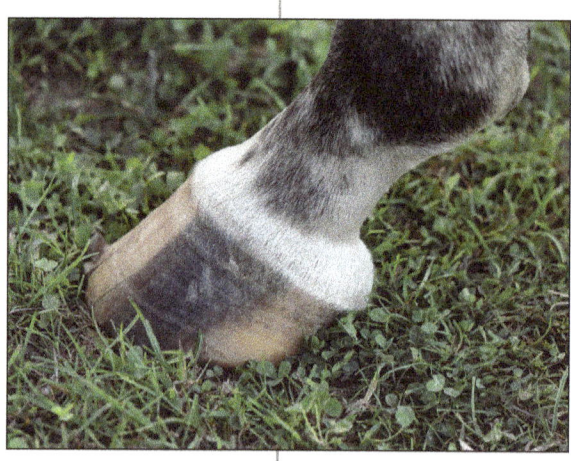

1. Coronet band
2. Wall
3. Toe
4. Quarter
5. Heel
6. Bulb
7. Small pastern

What Is the Bulb and the Frog?

BAREFOOT HOOF, FROM UNDERSIDE

1. Central groove
2. Frog (V shaped area)
3. Bulb
4. Heel perioplium
5. collateral groove
6. Heel
7. Bar
8. Seat of corn
9. Pigmented walls
10. Water line (inner layer)
11. White line
12. Apex of frog
13. Sole
14. Toe
15. How to measure width
16. Quarter
17. How to measure length

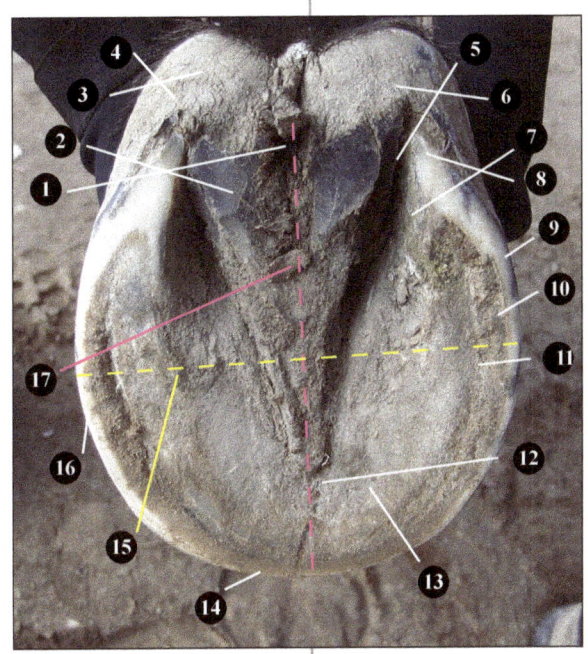

83

Why Do Horses Need Their Feet Cleaned?

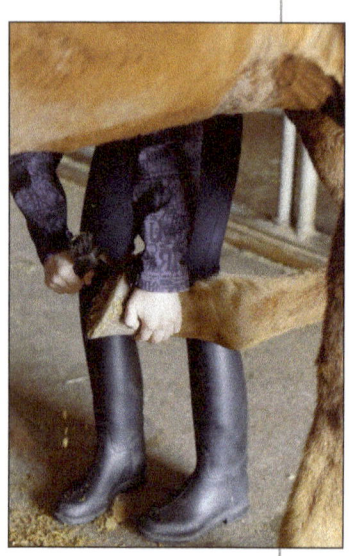

We examine the horse's foot both prior to and after any activity. This must be done to remove any lodged debris which can cause undue pressure on the tender sole of the foot. Since the horse's foot is so critical to its well-being, we also examine the foot often for injury and abnormalities.

Why Do Horses Wear Shoes?

Since the twelfth century we have nailed iron shoes on horses' hooves. The purpose is to hold the hoof wall together and to prevent wear and chipping of the thick horny covering. Nails do not hurt because the hoof wall is made of keratin and has no nerve endings, much like our fingernails. Shoes are changed about every five weeks.

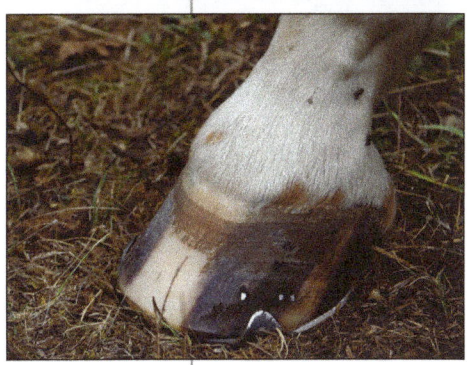

Who Is the Farrier?

A farrier is the person who trims the horse's feet and puts shoes on horse.

Why Do Carriage Drivers Put Blinkers on Horses?

- Blinkers block the horse's peripheral vision and keep them focused on their work.
- Blinkers prevent them from being distracted by scary things.
- Blinkers prevent horses from anticipating the signal of the whip.

Ms. Austin driving her PRE team at the Elms in Newport, RI.

How Much Can a Horse Carry or Pull?

- A horse can carry up to 20% of its weight. A thousand-pound horse can easily carry 200 pounds.
- A horse can pull a wheeled vehicle up to twice its weight. A thousand pound horse can pull up to 2,000 pounds.
- A pair of Belgian horses can drag along the ground up to 4,500 pounds.

How Much Do Horses Weigh?

- Light horses stand 14-16 hands high and average 840 to 1,200 pounds.
- Draft horses are often above 2,000 pounds.
- Horse feed companies offer scales and measuring tapes to determine weight.
- Each horse has its own ideal performance weight.

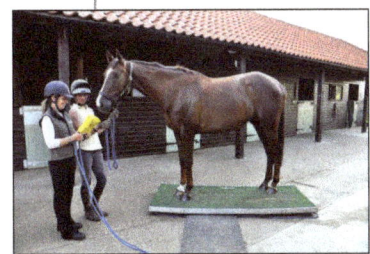

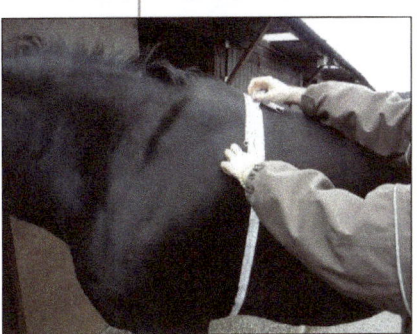

How Do You Measure a Horse's Height?

- To find a horse's height, measure from the ground to the highest point on the horse's withers (the last hair on a horses mane).
- Divide the number of inches by 4 to determine hands high, any decimals must be converted to inches.

Example:
64" = 16 hh (hands high)
65" = 16.1 hh
66" = 16.2
67" = 16.3
68" = 17hh

Why Are Horses Measured in Hands?

The height of horses is usually measured at the highest point of the withers, where the neck meets the back.

- The notation for this measure is hh – meaning 'h'ands 'h'igh.
- Used throughout history, because measuring devices were not readily available.
- A 15.2hh horse would measure 62 inches. 15 x 4 = 60 +2 = 62"

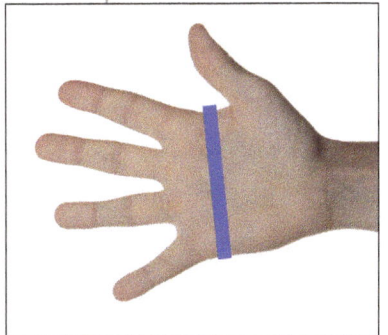

1 "Hand" = 4 inches

How Do You Estimate a Horse's Weight?

- Measure its heart girth and its length.
- Heart girth x heart girth x length, divided by 300, Plus 50 = weight.

Example:
77 x 77 x 66 divided by 300 + 50
= 1354.38 pounds

Heart Girth

Length

Where is the Weight and Balance of a Horse

- The horse's weight is distributed over its haunches and forehand. Because of the heavy head and neck, the horse carries a greater amount of weight on its forehand. When in motion, the horse uses its head and neck to influence its balance.

- 90% of the balance is in the head and neck.

- 60% of the weight is in front of the girth.

What is a "Horse Whisperer"?

Horse Whispers were successful trainers of horses, especially troubled or "problem" horses. The term may have originated with Irish horse trainer, Daniel Sullivan who stood facing the horse, close to its head and seemed to be whispering to it. In the times of trade guilds and "secret societies" in Great Britain, tradesmen and trainers wanted to keep their knowledge and methods from becoming widely known. Thus, the trainers with this specialized horse training skill set, became known as "Horse Whisperers."

Daniel Sullivan, the famed horse whisperer of Ireland, portrayed by Harrison Weir (1824-1906)

Who Was the Horse Whisperer of the 1800s?

John Solomon Rarey was well known for rehabilitating abused and vicious horses. From Groveport, Ohio, he authored "The Complete Horse Tamer" in 1862.

John Solomon Rarey. Photograph by Clarkington & Co. Credit: Wellcome Collection. Attribution 4.0 International (CC BY 4.0)

Rarey and the Queen's Horses

Credit: John Solomon Rarey with the stallion 'Cruiser', observed by onlookers. Wood engraving by Swain after J. Leech, 1858. Credit: Wellcome Collection. Attribution 4.0 International (CC BY 4.0)

Queen Victoria invited Rarey to a royal wedding where he entertained guests by tying and putting a wild, savage horse on the ground and then lying his head on its hooves.

In excerpt from Nicholas Evans' The Horse Whisperer, he describes Rarey's gentling of Cruiser, queen Victoria's rogue racehorse stallion by spending three hours in its stall and emerging with the horse without a muzzle and "as gentle as a lamb".

Was It Really a Secret?

- Daniel Sullivan (died in 1810)
- Willis J. Powell (died in 1848) wrote a book, *Tachyhippodamia; on The New Secret of Taming Horses* to which John Solomon Rarey's work, *Taming of Wild Horses*, was appended for publication.

Who are some Contemporary Natural Horsemanship Trainers?

A few of the more noted whisperers who have marketed their skills are:
- Tom Dorrance
- Ray Hunt
- John and Josh Lyons
- Clinton Anderson
- Pat Parelli
- GaWaNi Pony Boy
- Julie Goodnight
- Leslie Diamond
- Monty Roberts

GaWaNi Pony Boy - Cherokee, is a Tsalagi. He earned his MA in Boston and is an accomplished writer and horse trainer

Is It True That Alternative Health Treatments Are Available for Horses?

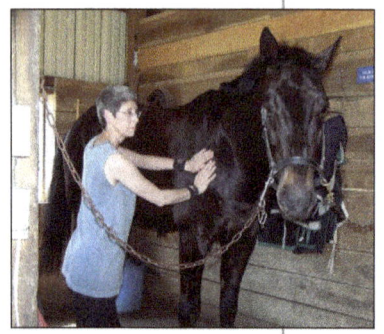

Sky Heartsong, Equine Massage Therapist

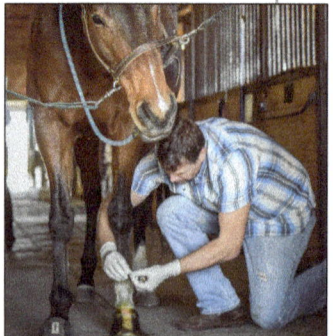

VetweRX - Equine Group

- Yes, there are equine dental technicians, chiropractors, massage therapists, acupuncturists, herbalists, etc.
- Veterinarians are the horse owner's primary source of medical care and information on nutrition and first aid.
- We have a shortage of large animal veterinarians in the USA.
- Other specialists are used according to the horse's particular needs.

Why Do Horses Crib, Pace, Chew Wood and Bite Themselves?

Horses are designed to be outdoor animals. When confined or fed an improper diet, they develop bad habits. Horses are designed to graze, play, sleep and socialize with other horses. Exercise is an important part of the life of a happy horse as well.

No horse is happy when confined. Domesticated horses adapt readily to work (riding and driving) if properly trained and they enjoy this as part of their day. Boredom and inactivity is a detriment to any horse and may precipitate this behavior.

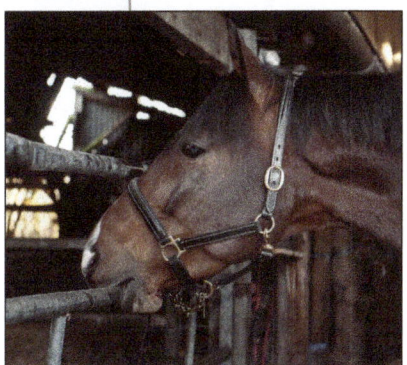

How Can Cribbing Be Curbed?

A horse's stress level goes up when cribbing.

Solutions:
- Cribbing Collar
- Cribbing Muzzle
- Anti-Cribbing Coating
- Change anything the horse usually grabs
- Don't buy a horse who shows signs of cribbing.

Symptoms:
- A repeated practice by your horse that includes setting his teeth on a solid object, perhaps a stall door, feeding bucket, or fence rail.
- Arching of neck to allow for the inhalation or sucking of air.
- Characteristic grunts or belching heard as a result of this gulping of air.
- The horse's neck muscles may appear enlarged if this habit is long-standing.

Why Do Horses Kick or Strike Out?

A horse kicks or strikes:
- when frightened.
- when they perceive a threat approaching from the rear.
- out of excitement.
- to prevent other horses from approaching from the rear.
- because something is happening in the horse's blind spots.
- because they are trained to kick.

    The capriole (meaning the leap of the goat) is a leaping and kicking out maneuver of a highly trained horse.

Why Do Horses Paw?

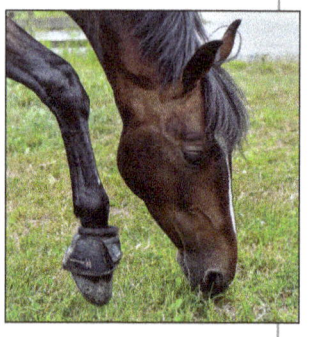

- They paw to test an unknown surface, to check if it is safe.
- They paw as play; often in water or as they ready themselves to role or lie down in water.
- They paw out of annoyance or impatience.
- They paw to strike out at another animal or person.
- They also paw to give warning to a predator.
- They paw to get attention, either from another horse or a person.
- Pawing may also indicate digestive problems, like colic.

Why Do Horses Buck?

In General:
- Excited, happy horses often run and buck "kicking up their heels".
- Bucking is a natural reaction to the approach of a perceived predator or a means of ridding itself of a predator that has jumped on its back.

While being driven:
- A horse may buck at an irritant or due to improper training, such as not allowing the horse to become accustomed to the harness and carriage.

While being ridden:
- Excitement or discomfort from an irritant or soreness of the back.

Rodeo 'broncs' are bred to buck and are used with bucking straps around the horse's flank.

Remember: A horse must get its head down to have the balance it needs to get its hind feet in the air and buck.

Why Do Horses Spook?

In the wild, a horse's greatest defense mechanism is flight from its predators; therefore horse's senses are designed for quick response and instant flight. Spooking is part of the flight response in horses and allows them to rapidly escape.

Horses can hear, smell and see far better than humans; however, they cannot focus on close-up details as well as we do. Loud, unexpected or sudden noises also cause spooking. When the horse's eyes change from monocular to binocular vision, the shift and subsequent visual delay in receptivity is thought to also cause spooking in certain situations.

Is it Difficult to Get a Horse into a Horse Trailer?

As a prey animal, horses like to be where they can run from frightening things, so:
- They are naturally claustrophobic.
- They don't like small spaces.
- Their eyes are slow to adjust to light changes.
- They are fearful of going from the bright light to a darkened trailer.

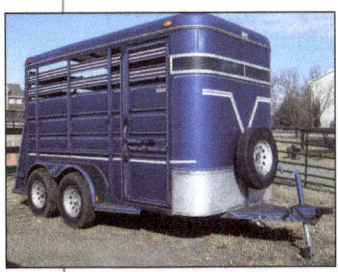

Some horses panic inside of a trailer, so learning the proper method of teaching the horse to load is imperative. We recommend a video like John Lyons "Leading and Loading."

High Performance horses, which are idol during transport, should not be fed grain prior to transporting. Long periods of inactivity, travel stresses and long hours of confinement in a trailer, when combined with high carbohydrate food stuffs like grains, can cause issues. Adequate hay and water are the best staples during trailer transport.

What Does Being 'Cast' Mean?

Rolling in a confined space can mean trouble. The horse can get caught with its feet up in the air and its head in a position which makes it impossible to right itself. The horse's head is needed to thrust itself into a standing position.

Lying on the ground propped on its spine can cause abnormal pressure on the organs which can result in damage which may be life threatening to the horse.

Extricating the horse should be done carefully, since they may flail and strike the person trying to help. When trying to move the horse to a position where it can raise from the ground requires pulling on both the horse's mane, (not halter!) and some lead lines or ropes around its feet. Consult a professional before attempting this.

How Do You Extricate a Cast Horse?

- Walk to the location calmly and talk quietly and soothingly.
- Loop a rope around the furthest front pastern.
- Brace feet against the horse's neck, if necessary.
- Pull and move quickly out of the way.

This often takes two people – one on the front rope on the front pastern and on one the back pastern.

*One should watch or take instruction from a professional on how to execute this maneuver before attempting it.

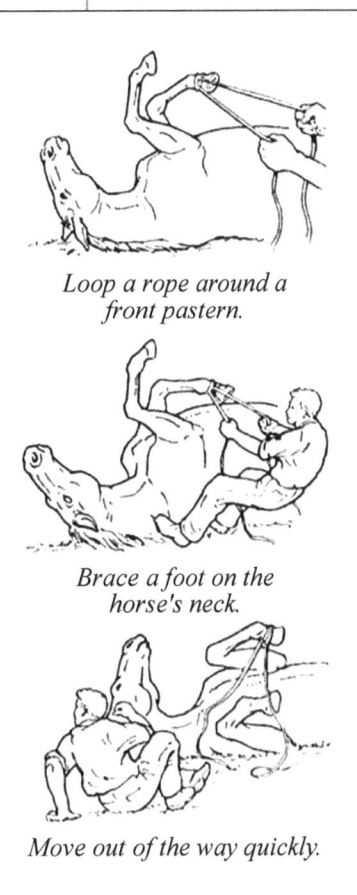

Loop a rope around a front pastern.

Brace a foot on the horse's neck.

Move out of the way quickly.

Why do Horses Return to Burning Barns?

Here are the facts:
- In a crisis, a horse seeks safety and security.
- For a horse, safety equals its herd, familiar places, and its leader.
- Horses do not have a good understanding of the dangers of fire.
- Horses tend to associate the place where they are housed and groomed as a place of safety.

It can happen. It has happened. Never let animals loose in an area where they are able to return to a burning structure.

What is Colic?

- Horses cannot vomit, burp or breathe through their mouths.
- "Colic" is the term associated with a stomach ache in equines.
- Gas or impaction can cause discomfort.
- This discomfort can cause the horse to roll and twist its intestines.

What is Sweet Itch?

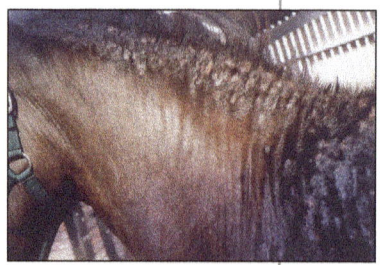

- Sweet itch in horses, ponies and donkeys is an allergic response to the saliva in the bite of the Culicoides midge (gnat, no-see-um, punky) and to a lesser degree the black fly (Simulium Equinum), horn fly and stable fly, which gives rise to intense itching.
- Sweet itch affects the midline of the horse mane, tail and back.
- Adding cider vinegar to the horse's feed helps with Sweet itch.
- Applying Avon's Skin So Soft bath oil, menthol products, such as Vick's VapoRub to susceptible areas, discourages the biting insects.

Common Ailments of a Horse's Skin

Dew Poisoning
Location: Lower legs and Muzzle
Presents as: Painful, weeping patches with thick scabs.
Cause: Certain plant liquids; sneezeweed, stinging nettle, and spurge.
Treatment: Wash with mild soap and water then dry thoroughly. Corticosteroids or zinc oxide ointment may ease the reaction.

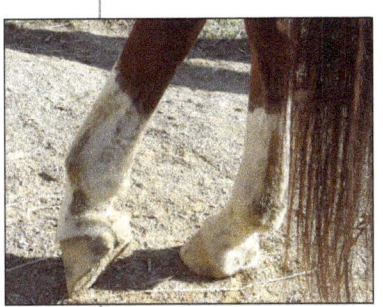

Lice
Location: Most commonly noticeable on shoulders and neck.
Presents as: Dry, waxy crusts, then hair loss from rubbing. Horse will be itchy.
Cause: Exposure to infested locations and animals.
Treatment: Livestock insecticide powders: apply to horses as well as to tack, brushes, rubbing posts, etc.

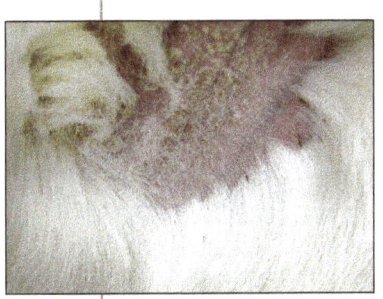

Photosensitivity
Location: Most commonly on pink skin of face, top of fetlocks, and coronary bands.
Presents as: Purplish discoloration followed by formation of thick scabs, painful as if sunburned
Cause: Sun and certain chemicals in clover, alfalfa and other plants.
Treatment: Shield affected areas of skin from sunlight, in susceptible animals, avoid feeding causative plants.

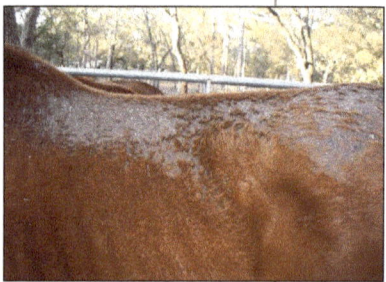

Rainrot
Location: Crusts that follow the runoff pattern of rain on the body.
Presents as: Scabs and hair loss with sensitive areas of hair loss.
Cause: Dermato- philus organisms; reaction to moisture on dirty coat.
Treatment: Penicillin; shelter convalescing horse from weather.
Prevention: Regular, proper grooming.

Ringworm
Location: Hairless patches with crusts and scabs.
Presents as: Little or no skin sensitivity.
Cause: Fungal infection, likely Microsporum or Trichophyton
Treatment: Bathe the horse with human dandruff shampoo.
Prevention: Disinfect tack and equipment. Keep stalls clean.

Seborrhea
Location: Waxy or greasy skin with an odor Hairless patches with crusts and scabs.
Presents as: Little or no skin sensitivity.
Cause: Mild cases cause shedding. Chronic cases are associated with other disorders.
Treatment: Bathing horse with seborrhea shampoo. If the condition persists, call your veterinarian.

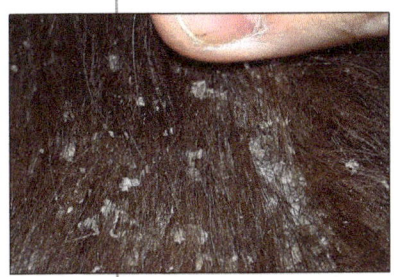

Sweet Itch
Location: Thickened, bare and weepy patches with hair damage.
Presents as: Extreme irritation and itching.
Cause: Reaction to Culicoides midges.
Treatment: Corticosteroids may relieve itching; protect horses from further bites.

What is "Rain Rot" in Horses?

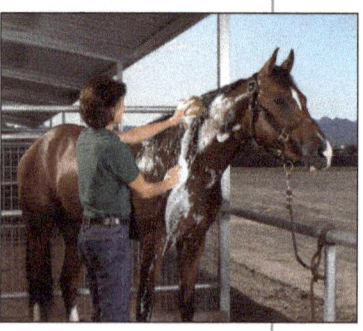

- A skin infection, sometimes called "rain scald," "mud fever," or "Streptothricosis."
- Rain rot is caused by the bacterium (dermatophilus congolensis), which behaves much like a fungus.
- Rain rot appears as crust-like scabs and small matted tufts of hair.
- Dermatophilus congolensis is treated with an antimicrobial and antibacterial shampoo, as well as removing scabs, and exposing the area to open dry air.
- The horse should be kept dry and clean, and isolated.

Do Horses Get Fleas?

Horses do not generally get fleas. Fleas lay eggs on the ground; and once those eggs hatch, the babies look for a new host. Since horses sleep standing up, (most of the time) they don't transfer onto the horse's body. If a horse is housed with flea infested animals (like dogs or cats), you may find some fleas on its body, which the horse has picked up from the other animals.

Horses can get ticks, however. Horses also attract many other creepy crawly critters. Horse flies, Deer flies, and Bot flies are just a few.

Horse fly

Deer fly

Bot fly

Why Do Horse Caretakers Hate Mosquitoes and Other Biting Bugs?

They are vector for the transmission of many diseases:
- Equine Infectious Anemia
- Vesicular Stomatitis
- Potomac Horse Fever
- Equine Encephalomyelitis

Why Do Horses Need De-worming?

Parasite management requires giving horses anthelmintic drugs. Common types include:
- Purge wormers (every 8-10 weeks)
- Continuous wormers
- Severely infested animals require daily low-doses treatments.

Worm infestations are reduced by:
- Removing dropping from stalls and sheds.
- Breaking up droppings in pastures.
- Reduced crowding of horses.
- Removing bot fly eggs from coat, skin and hair.

Worm found in horse

What is Eastern Equine Encephalitis?

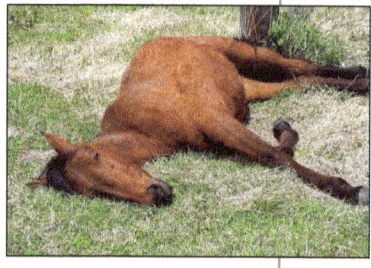

- Eastern Equine Encephalitis (EEE) is a virus sometimes called "Sleeping Sickness."
- Horses can be vaccinated for Eastern, Western and Venezuelan types.
- EEE is a viral disease of wild birds, which is transmitted to horses and humans by mosquitoes.
- The virus is found near wetland habitats along the eastern seaboard from New England to Florida.
- Humans cannot get the virus from the horse. A Horse is considered a 'dead-end' host.
- Humans only get the virus from mosquitoes which have fed on birds with the disease.

What Vaccinations Are Given Regularly in the USA?

- Tetanus
- Eastern equine encephalitis (EEE)
- Western equine encephalomyelitis (WEE)
- Equine Influenza
- Rhinopneumonitis
- West Nile
- Potomac Horse Fever
- Rabies

Which Vaccinations Are Given to Horses in Endemic and High Risk Areas?

- Strangles
- Venezuelan equine encephalomyelitis (VEE)
- Equine Viral Arteritis
- Botulism
- Anthrax

What is a Coggins Test?

A blood test performed since the 1970s, used to detect Equine Infectious Anemia (EIA), Coggins test records are required in many States and requirements vary. Check with your veterinarian. EIA is a retrovirus infection in the blood, transmitted in the blood, saliva, urine, milk and body secretions. Sometimes called Swamp Fever, it affects the central nervous system. EIA is transmitted by blood sucking flies, mosquitoes and other biting insects and is usually fatal in horses and sometimes in people.

How is a Horse Identified for Official Purposes?

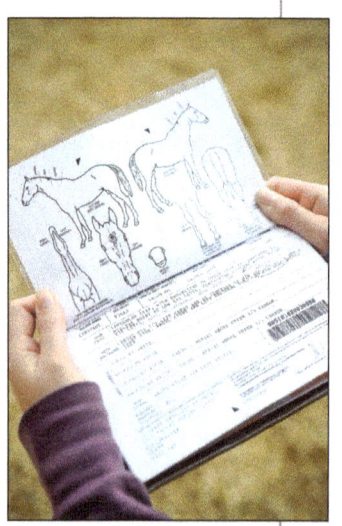

Regulations for identifying horses worldwide vary greatly and proper research is vital before transporting a horse across State or Federal borders. Most countries require horses to have at least a certificate of veterinary inspection (CVI,) and usually a negative test for Equine infectious anemia (EIA) within 90 days. Canada and the United Kingdom require microchipping and a horse passport and many other European nations are now following this trend.

In the United States, all incoming and outgoing horses must have an International CVI prepared by a licensed veterinarian and endorsed by the USDA. Horses traveling to European countries are required to show current USDA-endorsed international veterinary inspection certificates and test negative for EIA, as well as strains of vesicular stomatitis within the last 90 days prior to export.

What is Microchipping?

Microchip systems have two parts: a microchip, generally a radio frequency identification device (RFID) and a scanner that reads it. The microchip, which is small enough to fit in a hypodermic needle, is a computer chip encased in biologically inert materials.

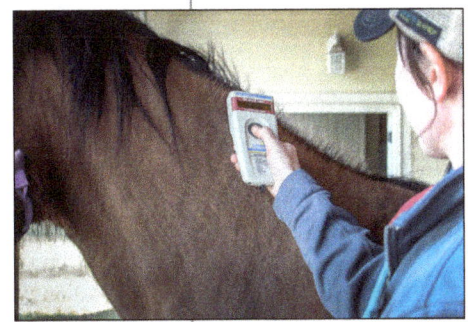

Each chip has a unique identification number programmed into it, which cannot be altered or easily removed. Injected into the nuchal ligament, the chip is guaranteed for the life of the animal. Several professional horse societies and many countries require a horse to be chipped, including the U.K., Australia, and even the FEI (Fédération Equestre Internationale) now requires horses in their competitions be microchipped.

What Other Methods of Identification are Used?

Signalment Identification - is using visual characteristics of a horse, including coat color, blazes and stockings, or coat-color patterns.

Chestnut Identification - is the use of pattern on the unique surface of chestnuts as identification.

Trichoglyphs Identification - is using the distinctive hair whorls, found throughout the coat pattern, especially on the neck.

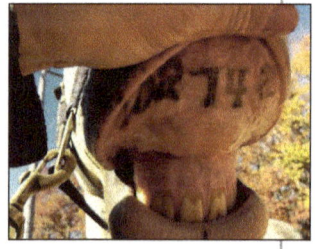

DNA Identification - provides a foolproof indicator of the horse. DNA must be on file.

Blood Test Identification - like DNA, this is an absolute test, as long as the blood is on file.

Freeze Brand Identification - uses a liquid nitrogen soaked branding devices to create a "brand" on the horse.

Lip Tattoo Identification - the Thoroughbred racing industry uses this as their the preferred identification method.

What Is Stringhalt?

Stringhalt is a jerking motion of the hind leg with involuntary flexion of the hock as the horse steps forward. It is called so because it resembles the function of strings on a marionette.

"Australian Stringhalt" is a name given to outbreaks caused by the ingestion of toxic plants. Removal of the horse from the pasture where the toxin is present may allow for the horse's recovery.

Muscle relaxants, anticonvulsants, and drugs that work directly on the central nervous system can be helpful for some horses; otherwise surgery on tendons is required.

What Is a Locking Stifle?

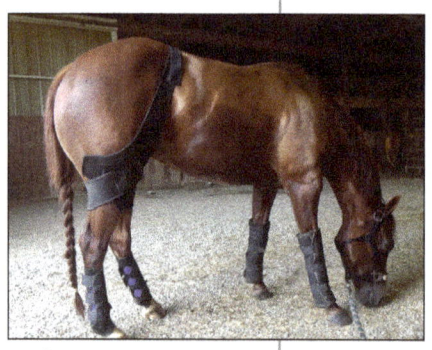

Stifle Wrap

The stifle is the largest and most complex joint of the horse.

- The stifle is equivalent to our knee joint.
- Gonitis (general term); is the upward fixation of the Patella or Locking Kneecap (specific term).
- Locking Stifle sometimes resembles stringhalt with a forward jerking movement.
- Moving a horse backwards or sideways may help to unlock the patella. You may need to also push in and down on the cap while backing the horse.

What is Roaring?

- The scientific term for roaring is laryngeal hemiplegia. Roaring is a condition that involves larynx dysfunction, which can severely compromise a horse's ability to breathe.
- The Thoroughbred seems to be the breed most often afflicted. However, other breeds that have the genetic tendency to be tall are also affected.
- There are surgical fixes; however, they are not always effective. A pleasure horse whose work doesn't call for intense effort may be able to live with the problem.
- When a horse shows any signs of difficulty in breathing, it is imperative that you contact your veterinarian.

Why Do Old Horses Get Swaybacks?

- As a horse ages, the muscles that hold up the abdomen weaken.
- The belly begins to sag, taking the topline of the back with it.
- The withers and hips protrude resulting in a 'U' shaped back.

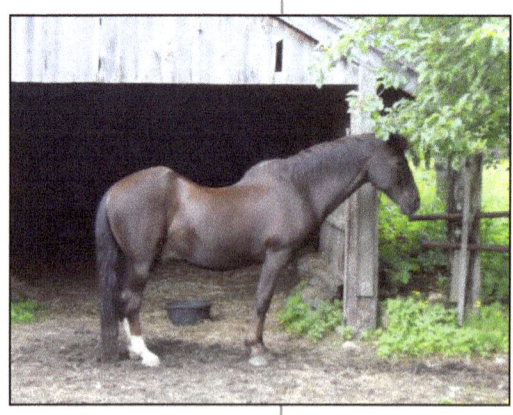

Why Do Most Efforts to Save a Horse With a Broken Leg Fail?

- Horses are large and heavy animals, as such; all four legs are required to support their weight.
- Their slender legs were designed for running and not standing still, which hinders recuperation.
- They don't survive well without moving.
- Stresses, even on a mended leg, can cause re-injury.
- Simply, the extra weight born by the healthy feet can cause laminitis – the separating of the hoof wall from the hoof.

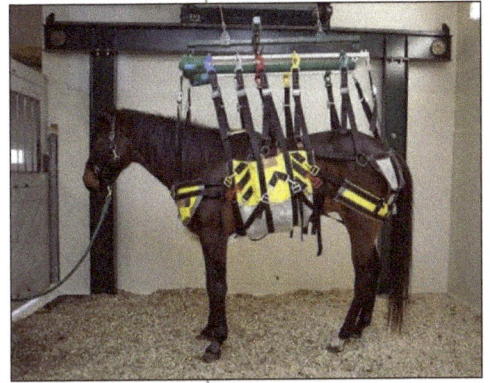

Robo Sling called Animal Rehabilitation Management System, or ARMS by RMD Engineering.

What is Monday Morning Sickness?

Equine exertional rhabdomyolysis(ER); sometimes called 'Monday Morning Disease' is a disorder which may occur in thoroughbreds or draft horses who do not work on Sunday and are fed their usual amounts of food. Signs of a severe bout of ER often include: reluctance to move, sweating, elevated heart and respiratory rates, anxious expression, shifting of weight from side to side, standing hunched and tense, passing of reddish-brown urine, dehydration, shock, and inability to rise. The specific cause of ER is unclear. Exercise, combined with other factors, seems to be a trigger. It is likely that several factors must act together in order to cause an ER attack. DO NOT MOVE THE HORSE!

What is 'Tying Up'?

- "Tying Up" describes a buildup of glycogen in the tissues, which creates an inadequate blood flow to the muscles.
- Mild cases present themselves as the horse being somewhat stiff after exercise.
- Severe cases exhibit intense pain, leading to an incapacitation of the horse.
- Common causes of tying-up include overfeeding of non-structural carbohydrates, under conditioning, exercise that exceeds the horse's level of conditioning, and electrolyte imbalances (particularly low sodium). Sporadic tying-up sometimes occurs in horses which have concurrent respiratory viral infections.
- Other names given to this syndrome include exertional rhabdomyolysis, Monday morning disease, and azoturia

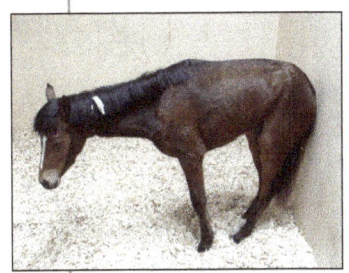

Bibliography

Becker, DVM, Marty. Why Horses Sleep Standing Up. Health Communications, Inc. Deerfield Beach, Florida. 2007

Budzik, Frances Mary. A Horse of Course. Metro Books, New York, 2008

Dines, Lisa. Why They Do That. Willow Creek Press, Minocqua, Wisconsin. 2003

Griffin MD, James M.; Gore DVM, Tom. Horse Owner's Veterinary Handbook. Howell Book House, Hoboken New Jersey, 1998.

Cowboyway.com Wikipedia.com

CATALOG OF GLORIA'S BOOKS

Coaches and Coaching Throughout the Ages
Understand what it takes to properly identify, turn out, and drive a coach. As well as insight into today's sport of coaching.

Carriage Lamps
What to look for, avoid, and how to use lamps with your carriage.

Dance! To Improve Riding and Driving Your Horse
Learn how the core of both equestrian athletics and dancers share striking parallels and how to improve your skills in both.

The Golden Carriage
The history & majesty of the Armbuster carriage. From its creation to its full restoration.

Hold Your HORSES -$28
Experience the Gilded Age of Coaching in one weekend. This event unfolds amongst the grand Newport mansions as they provide a nostalgic.

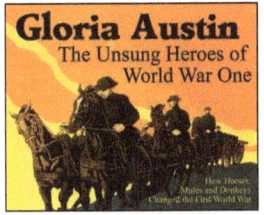

The Unsung Heros of WWI
The history of the WWI Cavalry was key to the war. Learn why war animals were vital to success.

The Medieval Horse
Dive into the various roles people held in society and the horse breeds bred for them.

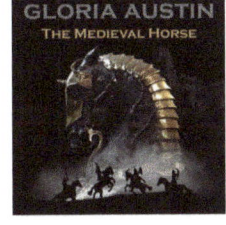

Horses of the Americas
Once a large population of horses covered the Americas. They dewindled, but now they have returned to the land.

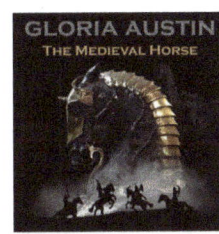

A Drive Through Time
A historical review of the use of carriages throughout time, from early primitive designs to modern elegant horse drawn conveyances.

Speak Your Horse's Language
Learn horse body language, communication, and social positioning, related to how a horse is driving.

Horse Symbolism
Travel through cultures, mythologies, and history to explore the concepts of the horse as a symbol in our lives.

The Brewster Story
Born of conservative values, Brewsters put their name and stamp on an era of great progress in America.

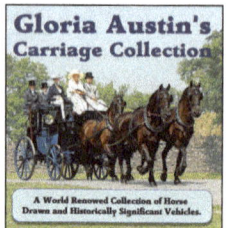

Gloria Austin's Carriage Collection
Over 150 carriages photos described for your review & information about who, what, when, where, and how of the carriage world.

Equine Elegance
Peek into the world of carriage drivers and their horses. See the majesty of famous and well known drives.

The Fire Horse
The history of the horse-drawn fire engines is rich with the greatness of the horse. whether it be a horse-drawn fire pumper of a fire wagon.

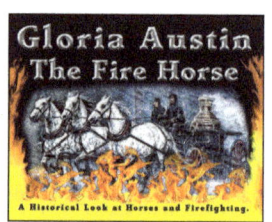

The Horse, History, and Human Culture
Read about the use of the horse from primitive hunter gatherers to modern day.

Westward Ho!
Learn about the advancement of stagecoaches and how horses were crucial to surviving the harsh journeys endured by many pioneers and travelers.

The Mighty Mule
Mules have played a key role in the development of the world.

A Glossary of Harness Parts
A compiled list of commonly used terms for the various components of harnessing.

Women and Horses
Meet some of the most iconic horse women throughout the ages and explore the special bond that women have with horses.

Coaches, Carriages, and Carts
Horse-drawn vehicles are the foundation of modern transportation. Come explore the type, use, design, and industry of coaches and carriages.

The American Horse
From the settling of the country to the surrender at Yorktown - that gave America its independence - to the westward expansion of the country and the rise of great cities, horses have been a vital part of the history of America.

Horses and Newport
Experience the Gilded Age of Coaching in one weekend. This event unfolds amongst the grand mansions of Newport with scenic drives on horse-drawn turnouts.

A Cookbook for Horse Lovers
This cookbook traces the history of cooking and how horses have been a part of that journey. Included are many of our favorite tested, researched and yes, tasted recipes!

www.ingramcontent.com/pod-product-compliance
Lightning Source LLC
Chambersburg PA
CBHW051357110526
44592CB00023B/2863